SEVEN

STUDIES

FOR

A

SELF

PORTRAIT

SEVEN

STUDIES

FOR

A

SELF

PORTRAIT

POEMS BY JEE LEONG KOH

BENCH
PRESS

SEVEN STUDIES FOR A SELF PORTRAIT

First North American Publication 2011
by Bench Press
www.benchpresspoetry.com

Photography © 2011 Stephanie Bart-Horvath
Book design by Stephanie Bart-Horvath

Grateful acknowledgement is made to the following publications, in which these poems, sometimes in different form, have appeared:

At Length, Cimarron Review, Common Knowledge, Ganymede, Ganymede Unfinished, Glass, Los Angeles Review, Mixed Nerve, PN Review, Poetzine, Qarrtsiluni, Raintown Review, Shit Creek Review, Walnut Literary Review and *Zócalo Public Square.*

For Andrew

"And this is all my creating and striving, that I create and carry together into One what is fragment and riddle and dreadful accident."

–Friedrich Nietzsche, *Thus Spoke Zarathustra*

C O N T E N T S

SEVEN STUDIES FOR A
SELF PORTRAIT

Study #1: After Albrecht Dürer

Double eye. Double bind. Double blind.
The dark paints the dark in the dark.
I am the Christ. I am not the Christ.
I am not making claims, or so I claim.
So I watch my eyes, my eyes that work
in blue, in all that looks beautifully true.
When the doormaker throws the sun in
my face, and shows my eyes are brown,
you shan't take my word for it any more.
Word can stand down, leave by the door.

Study #2: After Rembrandt van Rijn

The guarantee is your willingness to make faces
at yourself, and to let the weather do likewise.
No plastic surgery. No wrinkle cream. No hair dye.
Laugh lines, you mock the sudden errors in the text.
The serious creases supertitle a slow crash.
This face is, you claim with a golden flourish, me.
Well, in that case, who am I? Who is this writing
about you, making you up as I paint, repaint,
affording you the best lines, begging a few laughs?
Who but this dour worrier is your dear guarantor?

Study #3: After Vincent van Gogh

God sank a mineshaft into me for a reason
I could not see in the coalmining district.
Coal dust ate the baby potatoes and beer.
When a man slammed into a woman, dust
climbed in their heads and formed a cloud.
I carried away what was mine, and burned
black into blue, red to rose, yellow to gold.
I burn a house and change it to a church.
I burn the fuse of flesh and my face bursts,
a wheel of fireworks, a vase of sunflowers.

Study #4: After Egon Schiele

Look at me, cock in my claws,
combcrimson from scratching.
Skinny arms kink round my back
but can't kill the screeching itch.
The hand can't scratch its bones.
I snap off the blackened arrows
but their featherless beaks stab
the crying katydids, their broken
feet catch in the scattered flesh.
I stretch the canvas on the rack.

Study #5: After Frida Kahlo

I dream I am a wreck of a woman.

I am not grand like ruins, I am not a broken column.

I am the traffic accident on morning radio.

A bus handrail is sticking in my uterus like a huge thumbtack.

My collarbone hangs from my throat like a necklace.

I dream a monkey is picking up bits of my spine with his pale hands.

The monkey is carefully arranging me back together.

I hear the Professor say the monkey is the traditional symbol for lust.

My monkey is very gentle.

When he is finished, I will take him to my breast, and offer him my nipple.

Study #6: After Andy Warhol

Why be a man when you can be a brand?
Be copies the machine clicks to the market
to compete against other copies for a niche.
Not Nietzsche but Benjamin. My fancy
education. My immigrant genes. My coming
out or not coming out, and other agony stories.
What are they but printings on silkscreens,
recognizable by the cock or the shock of hair?
I'm waiting, like a dupe, in a photo booth,
wondering if I would pay for duplicates.

Study #7: After Yasumasa Morimura

After strapping the tits to my cricket chest
and pulling the famous hair over my scalp,
I talk to Marilyn about loving Art, playing
dumb blonde, being closeted as one thing.

She answers, with a toss of her head,
her nipples erect as the stalk of a fruit,
Grab me.

          I demur. Soft from politeness
or fear or disbelief.

               She takes my hands
by the wrists, presses them between her
thighs. *Now we can talk about anything.*

PROFILES

He Went

At first he went to Cairo for the lads,
whom he saw from his hotel window
passing through the market stalls
like unacknowledged gods.
Then he found himself
passing for a local, winning
the confidence of the blacktoothed elders,
uttering an automatic
prayer when the minaret floated
its call. He knew
he could never be a Muslim,
but he loved the religion's seriousness,
the gravity
in the brown eyes of his lover
who stepped out of a starry robe
to climb under his covers.

He Liked

He liked sunbathing on Christopher Street pier
where other sunbathers slept on the grass
like so many fish. He liked the idea
they were happy out of
water.
The grass blades bristled, the ants
with their busy jaws scavenged
what the summer gassed.
But the bathers were not dead yet,
they were dreaming
of limbs and lungs,
and the unaccustomed sun of mammal sex.

He Had

He had a runner's build but hated running.
He rooted
his toes
into the public park
and grew from his fingers
rose bushes.
He would not run, would not
ignite his lungs
and raze the flower's thorn and leaf,
but let decay
take its slow stationary course.

He Knew

Though he wore the body of a woman,
he knew he was a man. He didn't care
to assume public privileges nor assert
private virtues. The knowledge
was not political, not moral, but tricky
like déjà vu,
flickering like memory,
and, sometimes, descending
like understanding.
Some of the men he spoke with
said that was how they knew it too.

He Remembered

He estimated the cab fare
from sugar to quietus,
and carried the metal sum in his mouth
when he took his first trick home.
He still remembered the man
had excellent teeth, and how sweet
the stirring, and then
the disappearing.

He Watched

He had been thrashing for so long
that when the divorce came, like a ship,
he had no strength to hail it
but watched it pass, and bobbed
in its wake.

He Danced

On the roof, finally, there was dancing
he danced to satisfy
himself, sometimes
with another wriggling soul,
sometimes with a
rapturous hip, sometimes all alone
above the drumming columns of a beat,
dancing and dying on his feet.

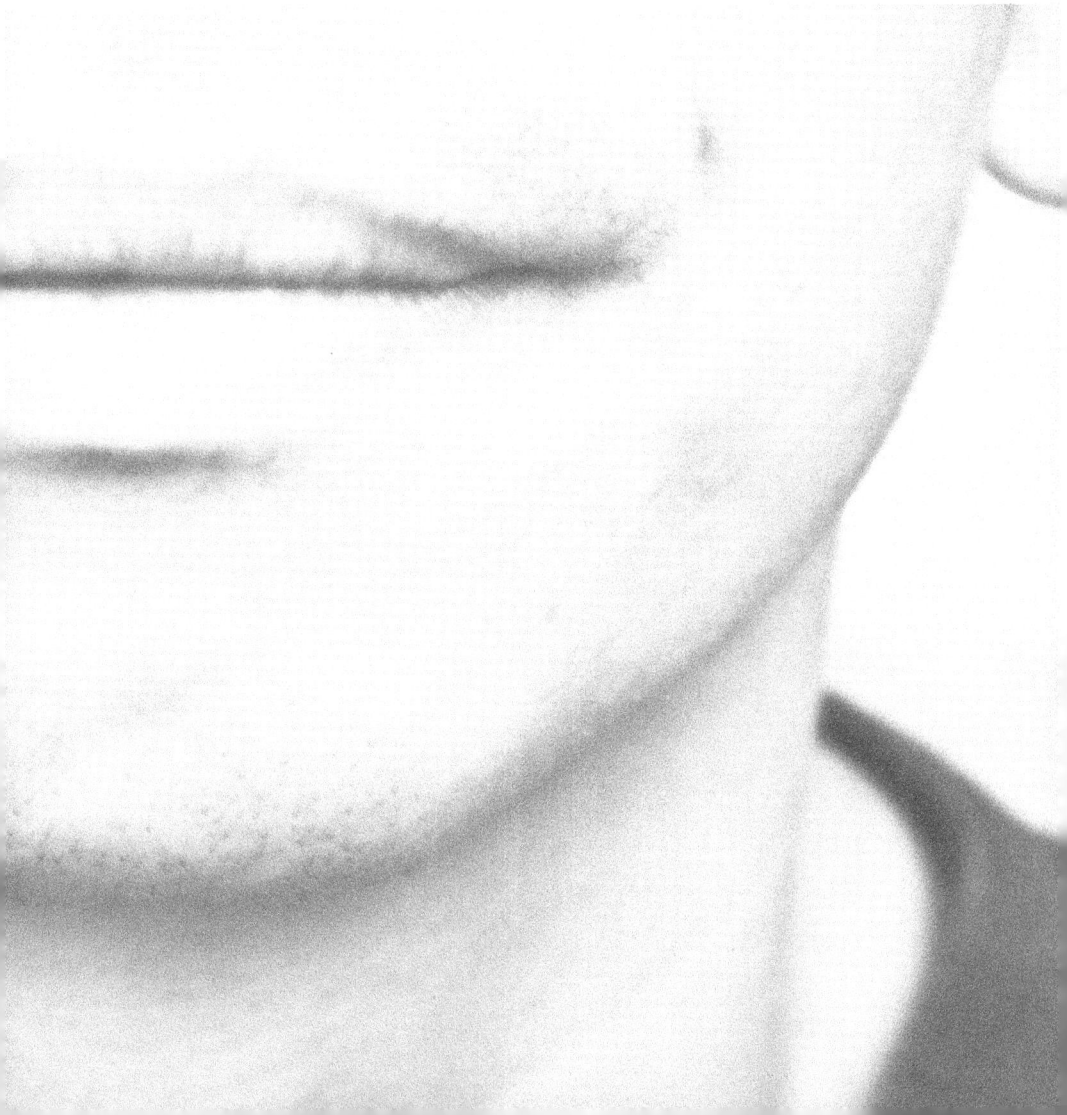

I AM MY NAMES

A.

I hear the drum of my father's life
most clearly when I sit at night
to type my poems of love and love.

His soft signal is growing soft.
I strain the harder to hear the drop
of ardor in the mountain air.

My name is Answer. I am a son.

D.

A thousand rooms wait for a call
that says they are a special space
and not a room out of a thousand.

Condoms confirm the poem's shape
the fierce cock disavows and breaks.
Between the condom and the cock,

my name is Double. I am a lover.

F.

I could not move nor take my eyes
from Shiva's magnificent butt
that boasts the beauty of a face.

When his consort opened her eyes,
she turned my naked impiety
into the first flame of the forest.

My name is Forever. I am a poet.

M.

The world is never what it seems.
It is far more interesting
to guess the secret affinities:

the boy and girl sleep side by side,
the lion by the slab of lamb,
the garden's promise by its rot.

My name is Mystery. I am a homosexual.

S.

What burden does a birthplace lay
on the shoulders of maturity?
What claims belong to a small country?

Declaiming against its measurements,
I learn the burden of its song,
and raise the earth into a poem.

My name is Singapore. I am a fulcrum.

V.

I'm North or South or East or West,
the bending rivers, the relentless roads,
or the broken skylight of a roost.

Old Famine brought me everywhere,
taught me to hear a fire's maw,
and answer with the tune of food.

My name is Variable. I am a Chinese.

A.

Each day revises the day before,
the riddle begun by baby talk,
the walk advanced by toddling aims.

The hands grow quicker than the eyes,
the head suspicious of the heart,
the body's ardor into age.

My name is Anon. I am a father.

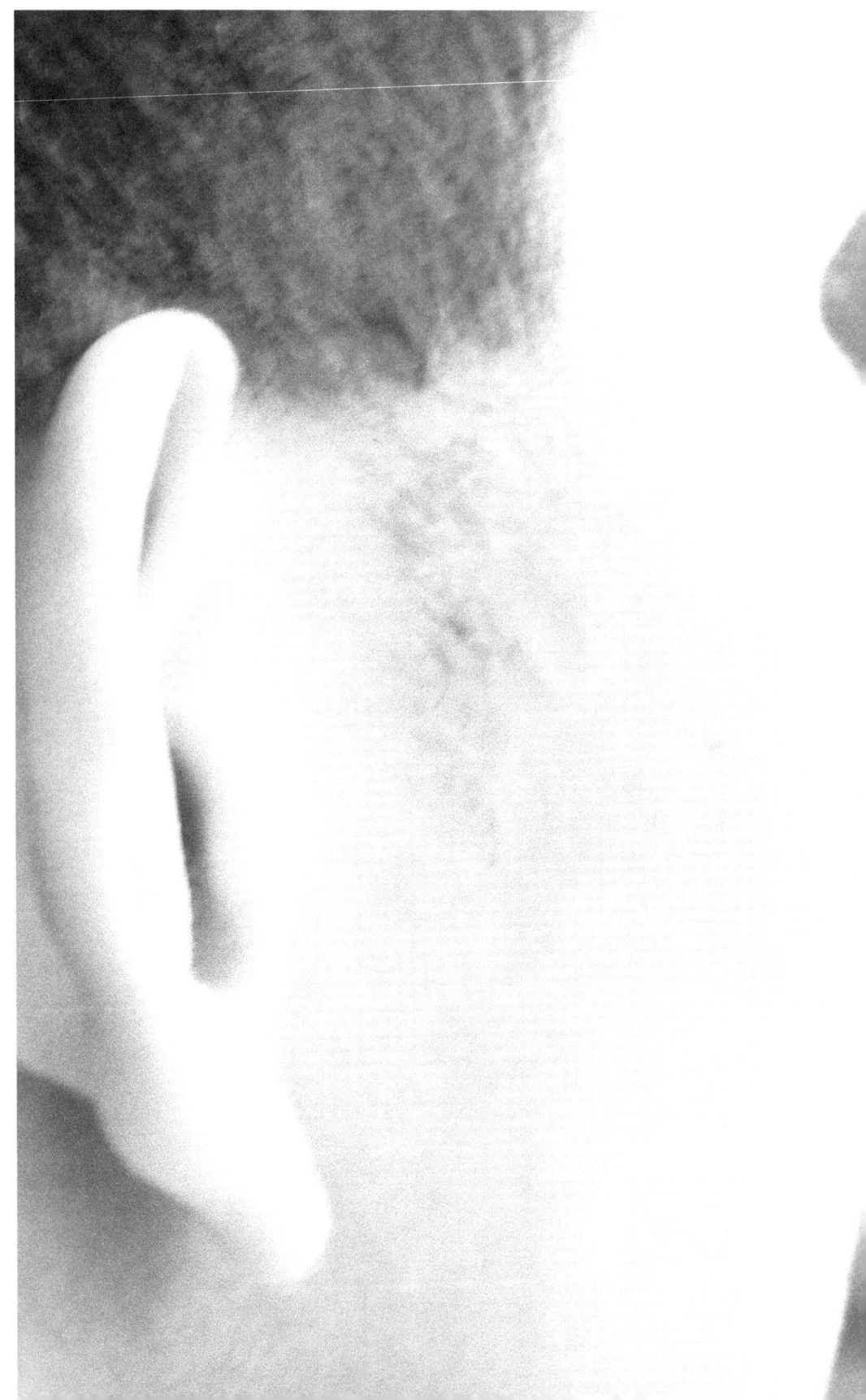

WHAT WE CALL VEGETABLES

Bud

Not rose, lotus,
delphinium,
nor aster, but

curtly called
cauliflower
we are cut

from flowering
and curdle in
a bunch of fever,

fractured crystals,
edible fractals.

Leaf

To make a living
we trade home
for sun, endure

the cold, adopt
Chinese customs,
Italian cooking.

Our passports read,
Spanish vegetable,
country of birth

unsure, Nepal
or imperial Persia.

Stem

We spar, we spear
softly, secretly,
your gut. We spare

most of you
our acrid smell.
A few get us.

Asparagus, Proust
says, perfumes
his chamber pot.

As do doctors.
As do saints.

Tuber

We sample Adam
and so his sons
name us yams.

We stem from hunger,
toughskinned, brownfleshed
God. We dream

of endless eating,
large and portable
power for good,

but raise a chief,
and then an empire.

Root

We sat for Cotan
like old grandees,
orange, skin

to core. Carrots
are not fruits. We
fire through earth

the green baize flare
flowering into
Queen Anne's lace,

and recoil
into the soil.

Bulb

When we unbutton
our skin, our whole
body slips through,

and leaves behind
more fleshy skin
for unbuttoning,

and skinnier body
for slipping through
the shrinking hole.

The rounded life.
An onion. A mouth.

Fruit

Ripe gulps of fat,
we bloat purple
in our broad face.

We boat sperm,
barreledcheeked,
and blow blood.

We are the fruit
and the bearer
of fruit. To the end

we bear sunlight,
we bear nightshade.

TRANSLATIONS OF AN UNKNOWN
MEXICAN POET

Unless

I'm going to kill myself unless the day lets me in.
Every face is a closed door. Every tree is a curtain.
The smallheaded pigeon brings no message for me.
The bright air gives way but doesn't give entrance.

I think I have been walking for a very long while,
past tall chain fences, down smoked church aisles,
round and round the shrinking circle of a clock,
away from the turn of cliffs that I walk towards.

I'm going to the Brooklyn Bridge, to stop thinking
about fences and churches and clocks. I'm going
to the middle of the Bridge to throw myself over it
to find another door since the day won't let me in,

unless some tree decides to raise its blind an inch,
unless some bird, perhaps a gull, begins to sing.

Marriage

I'm married to the Mother of unbecoming sorrows.
I approach her like one would approach a shrine
smashed by boys throwing stones for ball practice.
What has a husband to do with sacred fragments?

I'm married to the Mother of unbecoming sorrows.
The children eat from bottles while the bone china
rattles from the cool dark of the heirloom dresser.
Tomorrow, yes, tomorrow, I will trash the plates.

She was a girl, once, green as a stalk of grass
I held between my teeth. She was the dew, once,
translucent sun on the tip of the stalk of grass
I bit into. She was the sweet, once, in the grass,

now she's the Mother of unbecoming sorrows
I'm married to, I'm married to, I'm married to.

The Corner

After the dark has leaned in the corner for hours,
the corner of the kitchen where I sat to write,
the notebook opened like a souvenir matchbook
down to its last match, the ashtray on my right;

after the dark has looked for hours from the corner
of her eye, has looked pale, lovely, almost white
under her translucent sheath, her mouth a startling
ruby, her ring catching the history of moonlight;

after the dark has listened for corners in the hours,
has listened for the figure in the formless night,
the *ranchera* in the blood repeating its black plea
for an inhabitable country out of human sight;

I strike my last match and the dark comes to me.
The flame looks and looks, and then it fails to see.

No One

No one is reporting the mysterious package
left in the middle of the packed train platform
but everyone round the package must have seen
the red gift paper tied up with a thread of string.

No one must get hurt, least of all my Rocio,
breathing like a newborn in her big new bed,
white breast unbuttoned by her pink pajamas
and cupped by the night air's big warm hands.

No one hears the rattle, the metal rush, the brake
that powers the engines of my head, the crowd
driving from every direction towards the door—
body stiffened to a point—before pushing off.

Someone has to see the mysterious package.
Someone has to say something to the cops.

The Pocket

This house has not grown too tight for Juan yet
nor too last season for a new sense of the world,
but the discontented walls provide no pockets
for halfchewed gum, a shiny quarter, hands.

And the boy is searching for pockets everywhere.
Not the room shared with his sister, not the bed
which sheds its blue cotton skin without warning,
not even the body turning out its impulsive pouch.

Soon he will find the silver lining in the mind,
a seam we follow like a suture, then a scar,
and then an igneous ridge on which genius runs,
scrambling and scraping some, to the very head

and see the chewedup jungle and the shiny cities
kept safe and secret in the pocket of the palm.

The Pigeon

Even the light crumples in this city, let alone
the takeout menus thrust from street corners,
the flowers bandaged in cellophane, the fire
escapes, the fatlidded women on the train.

In some back kitchen the men are crumbling
a bag of peas into the soup. In some back alley
the washing machines are muttering distractedly.
The light is still trying to straighten its wrinkles.

This is not a rat ironed flat on the road. This is
a pigeon. See the wings flattened out to feather.
See the white fluff still not completely blackened.
Affixed to the ground, the animal ruffles the light.

Hard to tell the difference but it is a pigeon.
Hard to tell the difference but it is still bright.

The Night

The storm blew out the trees, and night became the night
all of the dark crossed the dark. The mountain heaved
to stony feet and climbed the straining rope of a track,
hand over hand over hand over hand over hand over hand.

The ground the mind rests on and dreams of thinking,
the water the river feeds to generous and gated pipes,
the fire the house subdues from lightning and burns,
the air the body breathes without breathing: all gone.

The mountain clambered
                                    and we hung off its back,
a rope curling from waist to waist to waist to waist
to an empty noose that hanged straight by its weight.

The storm blew out the trees, and night became the night
all of the dark crossed the dark, on Christmas night.

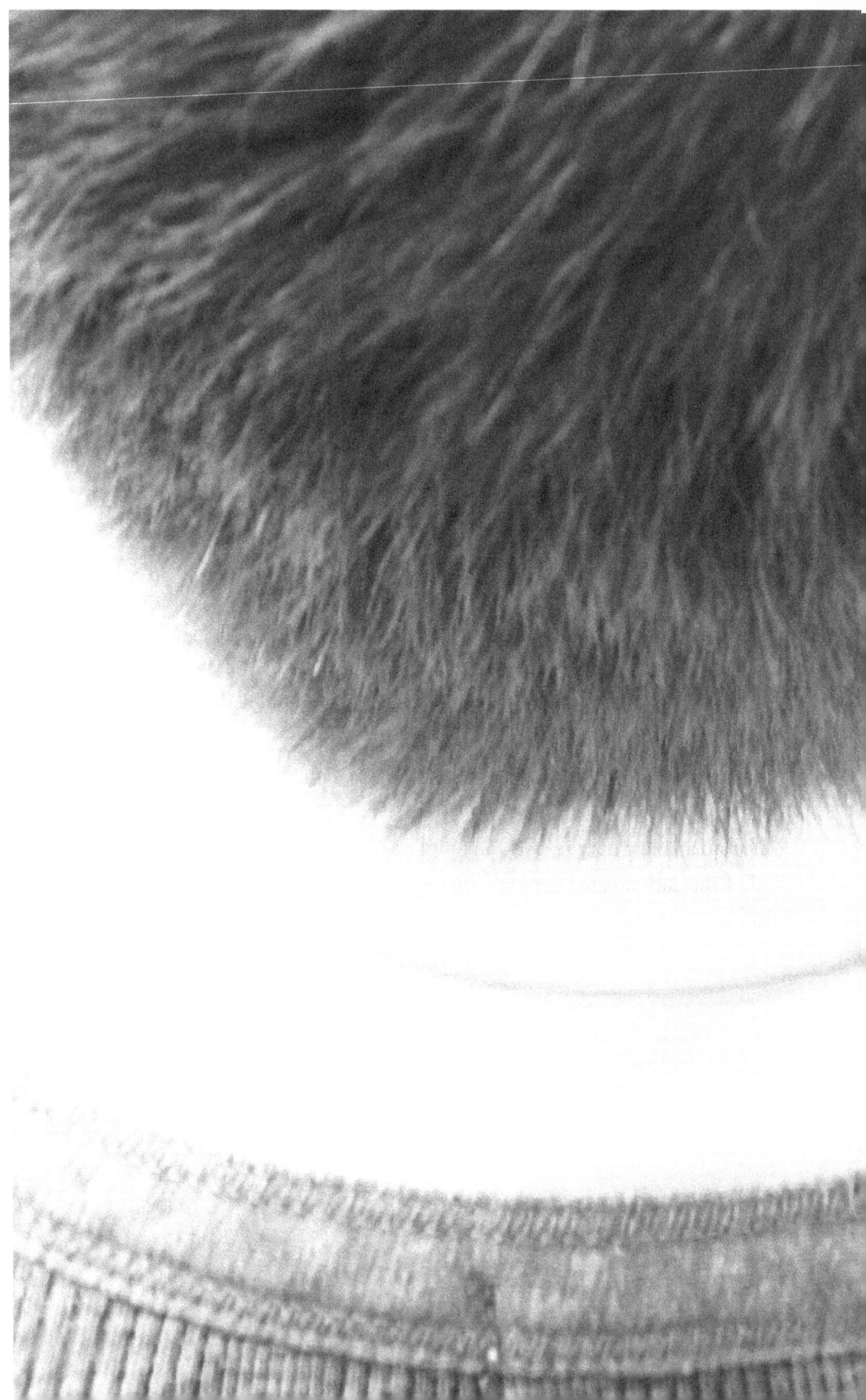

BULL ECLOGUES

"There's a part of my life that is so repulsive and dark that I have been warring against it for all of my adult life."

—Ted Haggard

.

The Cretan

You come out of the shower, warm and wet,
and towel your head with rough deliberation.
Those wide shoulders, untouched by a plough,
you wear like a smile, and the room smells right.

I know I should have sacrificed you to God,
I should have raised the knife despite its stone
and saved its bullion in your bullcow heart,
I should have turned from fucking with a beast.

Instead I let you lash my legs to you,
haul me through contracting caves, and grind
into the ground the altar of my lust;

yet, stubborn, round and gold, deep from the deeps,
the violence rises, the pressure lessening,
as if a ship is dragged up from the sea.

The Island

From week to week I walk on water, fight
the urge to look down at the deluged faces
whose liquid fingers prod my stony feet
for telltale qualities of softening.

When squalls rise up and shake the longstemmed brain,
even the faithful look for land, and land
their bodies on the strong arms of a beach,
the grass of books, tobacco flowers, night streams.

Turned, blown, off course, I landed on this room.
For here the krikri leaps with the white hills,
the citron bubbles in the hand, the olive branch

presented to a beast is not so beastly,
but promises a civilization
of the sea within, though not the sea without.

The Drug

Did you offer it first or did I ask?
Or did this ecstasy fall from the sky
and pulverize to powder on the floor?
We snort into the brain dead snowflakes.

This liquid crystal pumped into the vein
like lethal waste drained from cattle farms
is either nourishment or oblivion.
What speed does the blood crave, the heart endure?

Supernaturally heavy, hard and high,
alert to the nerve endings of your hair,
I don't confuse a zealous fuck with love.

I puff a cloud and change into a herd
my human senses and intelligence.
My soul roots for a cornfed meal, and squeals.

The Oracle

I want to tell you how the White House calls
for faith to light again the public square
and fight the culture wars: because of me
God has a hearing with the President.

I want to tell you thirty million heads,
chastised before the altar of great change,
pray after me, *Your will be done on earth*,
and watch the fire eat the ballot box.

I want to tell you all that I have won
but how can I? Outside this hotel room,
I am the man with no accent but God's.

Inside I have no language except lust.
Outside I shout, *God bless America!*
Inside my most authentic word is *fuck*.

The Maze

Some say the puzzle is the palace. Home,
its gorgeous wall hangings, gold passages
the hoofs stroll round, unable to kick down,
the kitchen an aroma of lamb stew.

Some say the world is riddled with tall caves
that beckon the explorer, strong and young,
deep into the intestines of intrigue,
and then the rectum's private resignation.

Between the world and home I'm lost to shame,
having given up the old habit, guilt.
What is this spool of red spun through the maze

I cannot say but see it to the end.
The ball shrinks fast. The pattern almost done.
Why does the wool look so much like a web?

The Cave

To be found out sounds like a sharp relief,
for godless enemies, but not for me,
the wide primetime report—ripping sheets
off private beds—of public sentencing.

Or else it sounds like holy disbelief,
confusion in the ranks, complicity,
on stony floors the awkward scrape of seats
pushed back, the quiet airconditioning.

At home it makes a smaller sound, the grief.
The click of a light switch. No mercy
in the darkness or the light the house repeats,

but hiding for a time, however brief,
in me, as in my den, I hear the plea
of an unfired bullet in the drawer firing.

The Brazen Bull

The thing I hate and love, the thing I killed,
erects a pattern for the spilling hours
and night that pours into the sprue and gate
sets round the thing I killed, the thing I love.

Breaking the mold, to see the thing I cast,
I see the thing's resemblance to the dead.
I look again, and then the face falls off:
I am the thing I cast, the thing I killed.

Where is the thing I love, I hate, the thing
not made by me, not made for me, not me,
some other feckless, soft and breathing thing?

Brass all, freezing and burning, is the thing
I enter as into my core and case
and entering it, the thing, I close the door.

A LOVER'S RECOURSE

After Roland Barthes

Take heart and sing of love's recourse: the river
is running from the river and still is the river.

A kiss in my bedroom and a kiss at the door.
The only French I speak: *be swallowed by the river.*

The cloudy pigeon, mutant dove, aches through the air,
nowhere safe to land, save the branches of the river.

You could not touch the other bank and so you thought,
a lake! It was never a lake. It was a river.

In the dark, flesh locates flesh with unerring instinct,
and fills in what it traced, the breathing map, the river.

Dragging for weeks his body for more than a body,
I hauled up a word—*need*, or was it, *feet*—from the river.

Someone advised Jee once to write what makes him sad.
She saw his whole life standing waistdeep in the river.

Say, mouth, what happened to the Riesling in the glass?
He kissed me twice. My tongue will not let go the glass.

The wanting hard, the losing, or the death of want:
to which catastrophe does your hand raise a glass?

His beautiful neck was strong as a piece of rope
by which he raised his head so slowly from his glass.

My hours are filled to the brim with his absence.
There is no more room for the elbow in the glass.

His torso poured a sparkling white into his legs
the way a bottle is intended for a glass.

The heart is finally a form of repetition.
We flip the body to restart the hourglass.

It's time to shut up, Jee, and sink your nose in wine.
You don't know yet the taste of drowning in a glass.

Even the siren, pushing routine off the road,
must travel by the highway code to gain its road.

The campfire dimmed the school buildings round it.
The stack of wood, kerosene soaked, smelled of the road.

The east may ride the prospector into the west,
but night exchanges with the day a ring of road.

Flying from the gun, the bullet fired by the gun.
You try hard not to think of him while on the road.

The road that underwrites a way out of repeat,
when you look for it, looks like any other road.

He has become the small country you imagine
leaving behind. He is the country and the road.

The sea turns in your blood but your nose lives on land.
So drink up, Jee, drink up, and one more for the road.

Pull the drawstring to close the sea into a lake.
The sea is wild but one can walk around the lake.

This small country is famous for its new bird park.
Wings clipped, the pink flamingoes flower on the lake.

These birds of paradise are trimmed to map the walks
so that their solar flares direct you to the lake.

A naked flame is dangerous. Replace the candle
with an oriole and hang the lantern over the lake.

The eye sees everything else at a proper distance.
The weathered sign says fortyfive miles to the lake.

The lover stands in no location but his feet.
He is close to the lake. The lover is the lake.

To see flamingoes, flowers, flames as forms of sea,
you must strip to the skin and enter, Jee, the lake.

God introduced himself to Adam with a finger.
All of Adam stumbled forth to meet in his finger.

My eyes are hooks but cannot hold his body's hem.
If only I could get close and catch with my fingers.

What word can bottle the sweet crush of his mouth
when grapefruit spills down the bevel of my fingers?

If the animals are to be saved in seven pairs,
the ark will learn to count on human limbs and fingers.

Watch me, Dad, watch me. I can hold my breath in water,
my mouth plugged by a cock, my nose and ass by fingers.

Two civilizations meet at the island's throat.
To my exterminator I bring a necklace of fingers.

Although Jee wishes for your arms to hold him close,
he will welcome your fading hands, or jittery fingers.

I see I am the last man drinking in the bar.
I vowed I'd never be the last man in a bar.

The drag queens, the pickups, the daddies and their sons
heard the night calling, *it's time!* and left the bar.

The ugly gogo dancer with the monstrous schlong
has vanished with his wad of dollars from the bar.

Even Freddy is not coming back from his break
to pour last shots, drink up, and talk trash at the bar.

You're lost. You're lost to me. Happy or sad somewhere.
You do not think to think I'm waiting in a bar.

This music stabs and stops the heart. The line is flat
although the rhythm is still six beats to the bar.

I would kiss myself if I could. (Stop crying, Jee.)
If I knew how or why, my mouth would close the bar.

The body drives so deeply in desire's cave
I revel in abrading skin against the cave.

I see the image of my pain in glittering things,
carry the treasures off and stock them in a cave.

On equatorial beaches that were once a home
I did not build a castle but I dug a cave.

My hands reach out and see nothing in the dark.
I console my heart there is an end to cave.

A valley drops away. A plain levels us all.
I love the tallness of my singing in a cave.

Then I remember you, your wide mouth, your high head,
and I suffer again the suffering of the cave.

Why does this lover's song always end with my name?
Why do you, Jee, count out your days inside a cave?

So soft his neck, so distant from the thought of stone,
I am appalled to see it pass into a stone.

That night swam for so long and slipped out of my hands.
Tonight it is as clear as fossil in the stone.

I come from a small country of large alterations,
where stone erects no memory for passing stone.

Somebody is fucking somebody in a corner.
Everybody juts as if released from stone.

Why have you come to kill this mutant, strong young man?
Hack off my head, and I will still turn flesh to stone.

There is a shiny slope in things that lie down flat.
In all coming and going speeds there is a stone.

He is not dead, I tell you, he is merely sleeping.
The rest of you move back. Jee, roll away the stone.

Eternal recurrence in the figure of a ring.
Is it a wedding, planetary or circus ring?

A stone dropped in the water does not see the ripple.
A steeple struck by lightning does not hear bells ring.

On an abbey's lawn I learned to make a daisy chain
from serious young men stretched out in a scattered ring.

I often think I moved my life to the wrong country.
The call is not for me whenever the phones ring.

These verses shifted round and round a vast white plain,
have been at times the dogs, the cattle, and the ring.

One thing leads to another, as one day the next,
but there are nights that huddle in a fiery ring.

Sick of the road, he sinks thankfully in a room
although too much, Jee thinks, is shut out of the ring.

The square root of minus money is a movie.
Applying for a green card is not a movie.

Marriage is between a woman and a man,
Miss USA replies, and beams. This is a movie.

When the illegal dies in American detention,
his name becomes a number. This is not a movie.

The Terminator repeats, *I'll be back*, and back
he comes to blast the baddies up. This is a movie.

The country I came from has crushed itself smaller
by banning citizen videos. This is not a movie.

Two men walk into the officers' mess. They shout,
we're getting married! Cheers erupt. This is a movie.

Can't stay but I'll call you, a country promises.
Jee has been waiting since. This is not a movie.

He thought, *the sides are never constant in a door.*
The side you cannot see is the back of the door.

Someone can get easily lost in this old house.
Take note: the closet mirror hides a secret door.

The apple wears its skin so well—I mean, so tight—
I cannot find the catch to open up the door.

In this great city, where you can sleep every night
with a different stranger, every bed unlocks a door.

The curtain goes up. An old man hunts for scissors.
This afternoon the silk won't enter through the door.

All God's saints know that waiting is an activity.
The day is marching round in a revolving door.

So he kissed you again at the bottom of the stairs.
How does a kiss nail a man, Jee, to the door?

The body is rather small but it is all the house
I have, and so I always travel with my house.

First man I fell in love with lived in ignorance.
We walked his dog when visiting his parents' house.

I have dreamed all my life of living by the sea,
listening to the waves dissolving the beach house.

You said of your first love, *we brought each other up*.
I ached with homesickness because I heard the house.

I have objections to the institution of marriage.
I suspect efforts to turn love into a house.

Love is not a house. It is always on the move.
What does a lasso have in common with a house?

A long day runs its dog into the horizon.
Jee does not think a line can rise to be a house.

A strand of natural pearls? More like a string of beads.
These verses, smoothed by sweat and prayer, are Dolor beads.

How many kisses have I threaded with his name!
How many beds have turned into a rack of beads!

The costume green was awful. Obscene was the heat
till it broke like a string, and the rain fell like beads.

The tightest cell is loosened by the smallest entrance.
The boy brushes past the curtain of colored beads.

You have been asked to guess the weight of the pig.
The answer can be found in mummy's jar of beads.

The beads are pearls in this one sense: they irritate.
The brain scratches its ghostly grit and creams the beads.

What would you give these islanders, Jee, for a gift?
A mirror? A religion? Give them seven beads.

I close the door but the day climbs in through a window.
Other days long thought dead follow it through the window.

Mad with us—or with dad—you turned us out. We walked
and turned but could not see your face at the small window.

You wheeled your bike past the window, and Dad was home.
I circled, with metallic clicks, the five o'clock window.

The windows, grilled to baffle body, locked us out,
but a wire finger opened the door through a window.

To cut my losses I chalk round me an endless circle.
To stop the train from crashing in I close the window.

Inside the restaurant, I watched you hurry in,
watched you, first, through the window, then, without the window.

Jee gives his dad the name of love, his mum, of loss.
She closed the door on us but, Love, he cleaned the windows.

Are the two men fighting or fucking on the bed?
Are they two men or one? Is that a bruise or bed?

After eating, he walked with me back to my room.
He flipped through my art books while sitting on my bed.

He eyed the twisting figures as I spoke of Bacon,
the carcass on the cross, the bloody mass in bed.

We drained the bottle of Bordeaux between us.
Our shoes removed, we met fully clothed in bed.

He stood up to go. He had to work tomorrow.
He does not sleep very well in a stranger's bed.

My hands have painted this night scene from many angles
but have not grasped the violent figure on the bed.

In this manner he has taught Jee more about Bacon
than any body who had fucked him in his bed.

I am not surprised the demon's name is Knife.
I am surprised he works like a fork, and not a knife.

Maddened with grief, a man applies a stick of butter
to the dry place in which he will insert his knife.

Another man, soft son to a hard father, slams
his daddy's wife—his daddy's ho—with his pig knife.

Demons are so theatrical, but so is love.
We overhear our whisper when we hold a knife.

The black ram will never wash white, no matter how
many hours the silk handkerchief rubs the knife.

You can shoot a man who sticks his head above the ridge
but you have to close in to kill him with a knife.

Some mornings liquefy into mud upon the touch.
The sun today stages for Jee a thousand knives.

My bedroom turned into a mouth with your first kiss.
Then at the door, before you left, we kissed our kiss.

All I have in the house is an empty wine bottle.
It will have to do to substantiate our kiss.

What follows after the beginning of a theme
if not the complicating silence to our kiss.

Of the three light bulbs in the ceiling, two have blown.
I write to your mouth by the brightness of our kiss.

I'm cynical about love, you said, and the words
circled the contact of our heads and sliced off our kiss.

My friend, an accountant, asks, *you saw him only twice?*
But see the symmetry: only two dates may kiss.

Stay awake and keep watch, Jee, though the flesh is weak,
for Judas is returning with another kiss.

There is something double in me that loves a mirror.
I can tell its age only by looking in the mirror.

If you do not exist, I would have to invent you,
my rival, my accomplice, my envy, my mirror.

Not that the fire engine is anything like the fire,
but as the day is to the night, to me the mirror.

Sure you can handle me sleeping in your place again?
I hear him in your words. I see him in your mirror.

You look Chinese, black hair, brown eyes, smooth chin, and slim.
Right cannot be told from left—or wrong—in this mirror.

His first love was a Filipino priest in church,
Mine a white physicist. Our past is smoke and mirrors.

You speak so freely of a past I do not share.
Know you are in Jee's looks, his eyes, his sights, his mirror.

The wine has turned to water, then to vinegar.
The dumbest guest will know it to be vinegar.

Tell me you have not kissed another man since then.
May your mouth taste on every cock my vinegar.

A stone will eat better if seasoned in a sauce.
You let me dip my hunger in your vinegar.

I will say it plainly. My heart is very sore.
My head is swimming. I will write in vinegar.

I want to savor every dish served in the feast.
Why soak all, like the vulgar, in the vinegar?

A common proof of love, they say, is jealousy.
The Chinese thinks that rice invented vinegar.

Before and after hunger, a husband suffers thirst.
Sponge your mouth, Jee, and offer up some vinegar.

The slight curve intimates there is another shoe.
Where is the other shoe? Where is the other shoe?

The pier walks you to see the seals swimming in pairs.
They slip by on their flippers, are not stopped by shoes.

I will not settle down with less than beauty, so
I will go to bed night after night in my shoes.

It took me half a life to stumble onto land.
My feet, size nine, still pinch like brand new shoes.

There is a room in me, as there is one in you,
which admits only callers who remove their shoes.

An epic must advance foot by musical foot.
A lyric falls on the torn underpants and shoe.

How do I write about a pain you do not share?
You are not Jee though you blister in my shoes.

It is not true that what ascends a flight of stairs
must reach a branch of stars. We too descend by stairs.

I was so wrong to think that lovers will make equals.
A step is higher—or else lower—on the stairs.

Eager to bring you home, I thought only of bed.
When you left me unsatisfied, I thought of stairs.

You leave me in a dark hallway smelling of shoes.
Does a kiss make a step? Two kisses make a stairs?

Last night I made out with two men, one black, one white.
Wrestling to top the other, we rolled down the stairs.

I'd rather walk a length of town than take a bus.
Do you prefer the elevator to the stairs?

Love, your voice answers from somewhere, faint, powerful:
Stop running, Jee. Stay for the night. Come up the stairs.

To the new temple built with stones the hue of pigeons,
I sacrifice these seven pairs of feral rock pigeons.

Three roads crisscross to form a rightangled park.
Scatter sunflower seeds and they will bring the pigeons.

Although you can line up your ducks all in a row,
the plastic crate has fewer holes than there are pigeons.

Not only to the ancients is a gift a claim.
You know I want too much in exchange for these pigeons.

Choose perfection of the life or of the work,
cries the large angel with a soft voice like a pigeon's.

I pause on a small stage before a blank audience,
and pull from my white glove a charcoal black pigeon.

He does not wish to choose between a dove and a dove.
In Jee's ribcage contracts the muscle of a pigeon.

He has not called or written for more than a week.
Henry James, Master and Virgin, died this week.

How does this book, a biography, persist in being
when the biographer gave up his ghost last week?

Why did you hide your profile—mouth—on Match.com?
I texted only once, to ask, *hw ws ur wk?*

Henry James wrote Hendrik Andersen many letters:
rare, correspond, vibrations, prompt, neglect, once, weeks.

I should have written, stupid fuck, *hw ws ur dy?*
and now it is far too late to revise that *wk.*

I masturbated every night before I slept.
Meaning: I have been a virgin this whole week.

Last time he wrote on Facebook, *Happy Birthday, Jee,*
I could have given up poetry. If he writes this week . . .

When asked *your place or mine*, meaning host or guest,
I always choose to travel and become a guest.

The good hosts in *The Odyssey* throw a great feast
and fantasies are grateful answers from the guest.

The old professor bought a house in New Hope.
He has invited me to be his weekend guest.

A beautiful book about ugly people, you wrote.
No, not ugly, but weak. Nick "Indecisive" Guest.

You are so right to fear my suitors for your heart.
I will consume your house. I am the constant guest.

There are house rules for a vacation orgasm.
After I play the host, I want to play the guest.

Sometimes Jee is Odysseus, sometimes Penelope.
The Indoeuropean root makes us host and guest.

Digging in a bed of guilt, I grow marvelous flowers.
The trowel studies hard the language of the flowers.

The man, a teacher, had not been touched for a month.
I fingerfucked his ass while looking at the flowers.

My ass would like to think a knotted rope of hemp
does not injure the flesh much more than do flowers.

Love is a luxurious hurt and a limited choice.
I'm sorry, dear. Please forgive me. I brought you flowers.

This week I train hard to transform ghazals to gazelles,
to flaunt this handicap: fortynine names of flowers.

At four, the windows black, I labor to sit still
and listen to the sap rising, and then the flowers.

Look at him, read his poem, or Jee will disappear.
God looked hard and where his looks fell, there were flowers.

I am a stone. I am a weir. I am my teeth.
You are a hiss. You are a fin. You are your teeth.

The thought of tying you to the bed makes me stiff.
Your bleeding mouth denounces all my bloody teeth.

My jaw muscles clamp up when I sing or yawn
because, asleep at night, I grind my teeth on teeth.

I was not given a vote at my mutant birth.
Inside my juicy kisses hide my carving teeth.

There is always a shred of humor in the monstrous.
There is a bone of laughter cracked between the teeth.

I have been working out to build up muscle mass
but they say you can tell a good horse by its teeth.

Many men compliment Jee on his sweet smile.
They do not stay for long. I have my father's teeth.

My horse is massive white. My flag is also white.
The star I wear inside my chest is flaming white.

First love, the physicist, went by the name of Strange.
He will still be a stranger when my hair turns white.

How do you like your eggs? Sunny side up, please.
The slurpy yellow set off by the crispy white.

Allergic to flowers, he hangs photographs of lilies.
His rooms are painted green. I remember them as white.

You know the magazine by its blood red frame.
You know the men you open up have skin called white.

They sailed back after noon with bass and fluke and blue.
We tasted the Atlantic, flesh so sweet and white.

To apprehend every multicolored flickering thing,
refract, Jee, through two densities the passing white.

You look into a stone and see its early fire.
You look into a fire and all you see is fire.

The reason that we saw each other only twice
is that I have no hands to thrust into the fire.

Time is a river. That is if you are a fish.
If you are a sunflower, time is a fire.

We do not ever know what the gods want of us.
Perhaps that is why we compare them to fire.

A charred library is sadder than a pile of ash.
A body catches but it does not cage a fire.

Saying it makes no difference to the universe
but when did saying anything put out a fire?

Sick of analogies, Jee wants the thing itself.
What are you, Love, when you are not a fire?

The strongarmed angel left and leaves behind a wound
that tears the heart but looks nothing like a wound.

Daubing a hurt with yellow medicine, my mother
minted a gold coin of the skin. I hoard these wounds.

Sometimes I am so satisfied to be a man,
I forget to raise the colors and salute my wounds.

The soldiers grip each other tight. Ejaculate.
Keep still. To pull apart will open up the wound.

The world, holding so many things, so many nothings,
is best represented by the body and its wounds.

When I think I can live with being queer all my life,
a morning happens, and the scar unlocks the wound.

Increscunt animi, virescit volnere vitus, Jee.
Spirits increase, and vigor grows, through a wound.

I shuddered, surprised, when you took me in your mouth.
It was as if you took my cock and not my mouth.

A shudder is a premonition of suffering
before my mouth surrenders promptly to your mouth.

The soft nothing of it! A cotton shirt against the skin.
Don't tear away the gag of your mouth from my mouth.

My feet may know the joy of traveling miles and miles.
My mouth prefers to loiter—totter—in your mouth.

A needle's eye is not made for a needle's eye
but your mouth tugs a thread and closes tight my mouth.

I have not yet described the treasure of your tongue.
I think my mouth will keep it secret in your mouth.

Jee was so ready for a ravishment and you
were ravishing when your mouth pulled out of my mouth.

Stop making a big scene about your broken heart.
Put it back in your pants, the soft and weepy heart.

If history is a roll call of military men,
the actor marches at its head, banging on his heart.

I am unmoved by daily pictures of the dead.
A poet sings of toads and strikes straight at my heart.

A porn star has nothing on me when it comes to pumping
the last reluctant drop of pleasure from the heart.

Was Sade outrageous about a turkey and a pope?
No more than fucking up a surgeon with a heart.

To be a pastry chef, witch doctor or double agent,
you have to be well versed in the perverted heart.

The obscene is a view Jee finds congenital.
Between a poem's legs is found a poet's heart.

I miss my train and end my travels in a station.
I cannot ride the whistling wind out of the station.

He had a feeling for vast things that come and go.
He came from a small country with one train station.

Today, like yesterday, work will be riding the train
from Woodside to the river, passing Bliss Street station.

The 7 train rattles my window at all hours.
A window is not a station. A window is a station.

My poems, I realize, have a penchant for definitions.
A definition is a small halt at a brief station.

I could compare my life to many awful things.
How else to wait out the long wait at the last station?

Wait, Jee, though the winds blow hard at this elevation.
One summary action will consecrate this station.

This house has no landline. It has two mobile phones.
Face almost touching face, we speak as on the phone.

My ears are losing your dear voice. You have not called.
Text messaging has nothing to do with a phone.

What tragedy can be averted, and what poetry,
if Romeo could get Juliet on the phone.

Last April Dad was diagnosed with COPD.
Freud liked to listen but he did not like the phone.

Once with a novelist, once with a lab technician,
I stroked my cock to their instructions on the phone.

We now suffer a vague continuous anxiety.
We do not lose but are always losing our phone.

You know the question when midnight abruptly rings.
Don't panic, Jee. It's Death, I mean, Dad, on the phone.

I pluck my theory of winter from the violin.
A lot of love is cold, so sings the violin.

You can as soon induce a law from idioms
as learn to bow by listening to a violin.

Last night the world fell back a step and bared its teeth.
A god was humoring a mortal violin.

If two French kisses do not constitute a proof,
then neither is a violin a violin.

To press my body weight past the point of failure.
To string you up and play you like a violin.

A trumpet is a hunter. A bassoon buffoon.
What human violations sound the violin?

So many things inspire Jee to sing but you
transform desire's voice into a violin.

Morning I sat in bed and opened up a book,
put it down, picked another, put down a fourth book.

Iowa decides for gay marriage today.
So proud of his home state, he writes on Facebook.

The sun is shining but I am in shadow here.
The bulk has fallen from the binding of the book.

What can I say to you? How will you take my words?
The real question: how does alone advance our book?

There was too little to begin with. (Or too much.)
Two dates are not enough for writing a good book.

That is the lesson of the sun. Except the nights
instruct me how to press the sun into my book.

Because I dare not tell you, Love, what possesses Jee,
my heart has written up my suffering in a book.

I was so proud to keep my garden free of gold
but creeping age has grown a stout regard for gold.

This distribution of the sun to those in want
I will compare to semen sooner than to gold.

Imagine my dismay, whenever I dream of you,
your desert image bellows with the horn of gold.

Late Monet glazed the painting of his garden path
with vegetable yellows and not with varnished gold.

When I am gone, bury me in a twist of myrrh.
Don't burn my body or my heart will show your gold.

My hands have learned to work in music, taste and scent.
Adorable, teach me to work also in gold.

The painting, finished, signed in the right corner, *Jee*,
will gather in the radiant godhead all the gold.

While I was scratching my name in the sand with a stick,
she said there are more than two ends to every stick.

In family altars, red and dark and permanent,
every stone urn insisted on an incense stick.

Modest by European standards the concert hall
flew me to the New World on a waving stick.

I was good at school and so I got the carrot.
The dumb, the willful and the odd, they got the stick.

Tramping up and down Lake Windermere with her,
our hands cut from the wind a sturdy walking stick.

Despite the sweat, nothing grew in the parade square
except the sun, the lapses and the swagger stick.

Nothing must move or you are out, Jee, of the game
when you reduce the homely clutter stick by stick.

To raise a house entirely made up of tiles
and to retain it after losing all the tiles.

Terrazzo. Linoleum. Parquet. Ceramic. Glass.
It is so hard to settle on one kind of tiles.

To enter paradise from Calat Alhambra
requires following the pattern in the tiles.

The proudest thing I have done for my father's house
is to replace the PVC with marble tiles.

He brings his body to the edge, and then turns back
to lay another fired tile by the first tiles.

A beach can be a grave but cannot be a house.
No reason, Sea, to line your mouth with fallen tiles.

If union is impossible, contact has to do.
An orchard, Jee, may grow from juxtaposing tiles.

Among the ways to take a good look at a tree,
the best is to lie down and look up at a tree.

I can no more hold you by naming qualities
than sacred names etched in the bark possess the tree.

All that I touch of you are touches and not you.
A torn branch does not make the tree less of a tree.

Your life—your speed—moves independently of mine.
Looking elsewhere does not hasten or slow the tree.

Being is your glory, which no one can take from you,
unless they take you down, for burial, from the tree.

The angel of despair, the demon of desire,
the many leaves that flutter on a lonely tree.

Jee, lay your anguish on the ground and look up.
The tree. The sky. The tree. The sky held by the tree.

I read *fulfillment*, and my mouth is filled with honey.
His cock spooned down my throat enormous gulps of honey.

So many nights surveyed the country from afar.
The settlement mornings deepened from milk to honey.

The man I lived with for a year laughs after he comes.
So much excitement, he thinks, for so little honey.

Every day I drink seven cups of instant coffee.
A cough catches my throat, I drink hot water and honey.

My soul will study hard the satisfaction scriptures.
The beaver will build dams. The bee will make honey.

Give him excess, for nothing quite exceeds like it.
Push past the point of honey, there pours still more honey.

Push past the point of honey, Jee, come on the hive,
the humming work, the stings, the wings, the hunk of honey.

Deep in your words, you realize you are your own father,
and son, beloved, lover, but most of all a father.

About this man whose kisses are fading from my mouth
I write, and make him up as if I were his father.

When she conceived of God, Mary composed a hymn.
Jesus' mother yipped when fucked by James's father.

The man, a big Broadway producer, spreads my ass.
I think of sitting on the shoulders of my father.

That these poems will not resuscitate the past
does not stop me from writing *once upon a father.*

The bitter truth is this: I write alone at home.
Here is no lover or beloved or son or father.

Here lies a man who sowed his words among the thorns.
No other children in the park will call Jee father.

No tropical undergrowth has stepped into a grove
but I think our second date is a kind of grove.

After two hours made love, they put on their shoes.
They are not allowed to reenter the grove.

The animals of thought are sacrificed to it.
My hands empty bowls of semen round the grove.

Repeat a word of power, like a ritual bird,
until the nonrepeatable comes from the grove.

When my body forces in between the trees,
it finds another place—a beach—and not the grove.

Before they piss, they ask forgiveness of the trees.
The soldiers know the nameless thing done in the grove.

Love is the name Jee gives to what cannot be named,
now is the time, and where he worships springs a grove.

In the cloister, in the Temple of the Sacred Fountain,
a monk is scooping up dead pigeons from the fountain.

Sick of the void, they grew a body round the heart
after they had devised a garden round the fountain.

Quiet evenings change the body to an aqueduct,
the phallus celebrating the stonework a fountain.

Night has come; now all fountains speak more loudly,
so Nietzsche writes, *and my soul, too, is a fountain.*

The reason a woman brings her buckets to a well
is the same reason young men embrace by a fountain.

The sound of my poems may be compared to a well's
but I would like to think they glitter like a fountain.

Jee, you may quarry from the sun the finest stone.
A form, without love's pressure, does not make a fountain.

Enclosed in the unstamped envelope of my skin
a seven page essay on the beauty of your skin.

My hands cannot surprise and so tickle my soles.
Miracles have to come from outside of my skin.

If one spear misses, number two will find its mark.
The scalp is but another name for human skin.

You have heard the unceasing roar of waterfalls.
You have not heard the volume of unbroken skin.

The state of Earth is not more softly draped with air
than this man's testicles are swaddled with his skin.

I grow hardest from making a man groan with pleasure,
from diving naked in and rippling through the skin.

As for your cock, Jee won't address its voiceless suit
until he has declared his force inside your skin.

So happy to find *anima* in *animal*,
as if you are ashamed of being an animal.

Man is as far from animal as love from lust,
the distance measured in units of animal.

How quickly I give up philosophy in bed!
As envy is to monster, joy is animal.

The mind thinks, *he would call if he were not so busy.*
I love you. Why don't you love me? cries the animal.

Asked to explain in one page what makes a great man great,
the boy turned in one phrase, *esprit de l'animal.*

A strong man stands behind every successful state.
Behind every strong idea rears an animal.

The Chinese zodiac says, Jee, you are a dog.
It's wrong. You are ringmaster of the animals.

You smell your fault as readily as you hear a bell.
Ignorance rings a school bell, ego a church bell.

The loop of wire moves along the twist of wire.
Steady your hand or desire will sound the bell.

I ache for the beautiful young men I pass on streets.
They do not know they are beautiful bronze bells.

Out of the party chatter rises a cathedral.
My tongue keeps ringing my head that is the bell.

He has heard of, but has not heard, the onehand clap.
He has tapped many bodies but has not heard the bell.

I hope perfection does not lie in quietness.
A poet builds his house in the fading of a bell.

The fading is a fault but silence is an itch.
Most unendurable, Jee, is the unrelenting bell.

If I should die today, the world has still its sun
and nothing is, I think, less mournful than the sun.

What is this world? A ship or a shiptearing rock?
And does the lighthouse look anything like the sun?

We met both times at night, on clear but starless nights.
I have not seen—may never see—you in the sun.

As far as poems are from person, or as near,
so far and near revolve the planets round the sun.

Because I have seen it since I first could see,
I think I know—poor fool!—the power of the sun.

I would hold you with such a warm and bright import
that you can say, when I am gone, *he was my sun*.

The source, the means and the effect combined in one:
these poems rise, Jee, with the rising of the sun.

To dream of union is to dream the world in words,
the multifarious world conferring with two words.

Pick up a fragment of the world, let's say, a stone,
and feel the heart—*hard* and *soft*—in the fist of words.

Lean on a week as you would on a stick. *So long.*
So short. We traveled here, accompanied by words.

When a backdoor is pried open and shows a cave,
do you go *in* or stay *out* of the ring of words?

You know the *ups* and *downs* of falling deep in love.
You know the stairs, that flowering tree, are made from words.

The road is for the wound. The knife is for the shoes.
The poem unites in time two dislocated words.

God breathed into Adam and gave him life at once.
You kissed Jee twice, first on his mouth, then on these words.

The summer does not hold on to love and it has love.
I would release him but what is holding me back? *Love.*

Shooting his load, the young monk keeps his eyes open.
Tell him, what is the white bird in the window? *Love.*

As Monet lost his eyes, his hands grew more abstract.
What brushed the water lilies, loss or love? *Love.*

The banks don't hide a wish to hold the river up.
If power builds a dam, what will a dam build? *Love.*

When Henry James wrote, "You have time. You are young. Live!"
what does the Master mean? *I think the man means love.*

Last night my ex fucked me as if it were our first.
What do we share when we don't share a house? *Love.*

Jee, the unlikely initial of God, you hope
so much for Paul, so much for Paul you hope for love.

ACKNOWLEDGEMENTS AND NOTES

I am very grateful to Andrew Howdle and Helaine L. Smith for reading and commenting on a draft of the book. I thank Sherri Wolf for lending me Roland Barthes's *A Lover's Discourse* at just the right time, and Jonathan Farmer for his suggestions on the ghazals. Guy E. Humphrey, for his loving support. John Stahle, who died in April 2010, encouraged and helped me to self-publish my work. He is much missed.

I thank the editors of the following journals for publishing these poems, some in earlier versions:

At Length: "A Lover's Recourse"

Cimarron Review: "Take heart and sing of love's recourse: the river"

Common Knowledge: "Pull the drawstring to close the sea into a lake," "Say, mouth, what happened to the Riesling in the glass," "It is not true that what ascends a flight of stairs," "The body is rather small but it is all the house" and "I miss my train and end my travels in a station"

Ganymede: "Seven Studies for a Self Portrait"

Ganymede Unfinished: "Profiles"

Glass: "I see I am the last man drinking in the bar" and "In the cloister, in the Temple of the Sacred Fountain"

Los Angeles Review: "What We Call Vegetables"

Mixed Nerve: "If I should die today, the world has still its sun" and "To dream of union is to dream the world in words"

PN Review: "Translations of an Unknown Mexican Poet":

"Unless," "Marriage," "The Corner," "No One," "The Pocket" and "The Night"; "I look into a stone and see its early fire," "Among the ways to take a good look at a tree," "You smell a fault as readily as you hear a bell," "I close the door but the day climbs in through a window" and "He thought, *the sides are never constant in a door*"

Poetzine: "God introduced himself to Adam with a finger," "The square root of minus money is a movie" and "Morning I sat in bed and opened up a book"

Qarrtsiluni: "So soft his neck, so distant from the thought of stone" and "When asked *your place or my place*, meaning host or guest" ("When asked *your place or mine*, meaning host or guest")

Raintown Review: "I pluck my theory of winter from the violin"

Shit Creek Review: "Digging in a bed of guilt, I grow marvelous flowers"

Walnut Literary Review: "I am a stone. I am a weir. I am my teeth," "My bedroom turned into a mouth with your first kiss" and "She says there are more than two ends to every stick" ("While I was scratching my name in the sand with a stick").

Zócalo Public Square: "I Am My Names"

→>→>→<←<←←

The book's epigraph is taken from Walter Kaufmann's translation of *Thus Spoke Zarathustra*.

Ted Haggard, an American evangelical pastor, allegedly paid for gay sex and used methamphetamine. Before the scandal broke, he was the President of the National Association of Evangelicals and a frequent caller at George W. Bush's White House.

Also published by Bench Press (www.benchpresspoetry.com) poetry that exerts pressure at every point, and so achieves a momentary rest

Lightly in the Good of Day, Bob Hart
Equal to the Earth, Jee Leong Koh

Jee Leong Koh is the author of two other books of poems, *Payday Loans* and *Equal to the Earth*. Born and raised in Singapore, he lives in New York City, and blogs at Song of a Reformed Headhunter (jeeleong.blogspot.com).

www.ingramcontent.com/pod-product-compliance
Lightning Source LLC
Chambersburg PA
CBHW071946100426
42736CB00042B/2145